Off the Beaten Path

Patrick G. Bryson

Editor: Cathy Lynn Bryson

Cover Photo: Cathy Lynn Bryson - <u>www.wingedprisms.com</u>

DEDICATION

For Cate Bryson
True Companion, Lover and Hopeful, Creative, Funny Best
Friend

FOREWORD

One day, while attending a conference for pastors and leaders at Rehoboth Beach, Delaware, I sat at a table with a beloved sister who traveled with me for lunch. This beautiful couple, glowing with the presence of God sat beside us. It was Patrick G. Bryson and his lovely wife, Cate. Immediately, we connected in the Spirit, as we shared who we were and the roads we had traveled. We soon realized that we were truly brothers and sisters in Christ. Little did I know how that first meeting would lead to over 15-years of God encounters. As time advanced, my husband and I were fortunate to have this beautiful couple stay in our home when traveling and enjoy dinners and prayer meetings together where God would show up as only God can do – extraordinarily.

As a former senior pastor of an inner-city church, Patrick Bryson became the prophet in my five-fold relationships and he and Cate are my brother and sister. Patrick Bryson frequently came to minister to our congregation. His love of God's people was evident and well as his desire to see the ears of the people open to the voice of God. Through his gifting, Patrick Bryson encouraged countless attendees with accurate prophetic words of encouragement, edification, and sound biblical teaching.

I remember many days of sitting in my office and my phone would ring; it would be Patrick Bryson. It is always a timely call, whether I was amid decision-making, dealing with disappointment or weariness,

INTRODUCTION

We want certainty in everything, it is our human nature. In time the wild place that an explorer discovered becomes a pacified place with rules, guidelines and laws to make certain it never becomes wild again.

God disrupts our well developed pacified environment. He speaks. His voice, the Psalmist said, *"breaks the cedars of Lebanon"* -Psalm 29:5. God's voice breaks up our familiar scene. Not only that, He disrupts our normal.

This book is an examination of one pilgrims journey to a Holy Place. It has taken me most of my life to recognize His hand in all of life, both big and small.

Patrick G. Bryson

CONTENTS

1

A CRY FOR WISDOM

I was a young pastor of a small church in a small community. The previous evening, myself and one of the elders had gone to the home of a church member and her unchurched husband. He met us at the door with threatening behavior and a visible weapon. He had not yet been violent to his family, but his behavior was paranoid and threatening.

That evening did not escalate and ended in safety and sighs of relief. However, it did cause me to think and pray in ways I never had to before.

That week I did what I often do to this day, I went for a cup of coffee. For some reason I drove fifty miles to a larger city to find a diner to have that cup.

I sat at the counter, my bible open in front of me, my first refill half consumed, when a well dressed man in business attire entered the diner. There were many open tables and booths, but he chose the counter seat next to me. Seeing my bible, he inquired if I was a believer and we spent the next ten minutes sharing about our common faith.

The gentleman, whom I have decided to name Doctor, and I then turned our conversation to our career choices. He was a psychiatrist practicing at a large hospital in the city we were in. I explained that I was a pastor in a small town an hour away. At this point, Doctor Distinguished looked at me and said, "Certainly the Lord must have a purpose in our meeting today."

I hadn't anticipated anything more than a bottomless cup of strong coffee when I set out for that diner. But now I saw the opportunity to find insight into a new and difficult situation my church member faced.

In a few minutes he gave me a professional, legal and moral perspective. Before I had a chance to consume any more caffeine, I had received wisdom from my learned and wise brother in the faith. He left before I even got his name.

The drive home was filled with thanksgiving for knowing what to do and amazement that my cry for wisdom had arrived just in time.

I reflect now on how several ingredients came together to serve up more than a bottomless cup of coffee at that diner, on that day.

- I had gotten out of my normal surroundings
- I had cried out for wisdom
- I recognized the opportunity when it came and I received it
- Just what I needed was served up like a slice of pie
- I thought I was after something natural, but what was set before me was inspired

You might think I drew too much from coffee and conversation, however, I find a Father who is speaking into every quandary and every cry for understanding.

When needing wisdom, do you expect God to come?

*Do you set limits on **how** He comes in wisdom?*

Are you ready to go "out of your way" to receive the wisdom you need?

2

AN EAST COAST DINER

AN EAST COAST DINER is a unique institution. National chain restaurants thrive on controlled portions and sameness, while diners provide you with entrees, sides, beverages and desserts for a reasonable price for the large portions they serve.

I was in central Pennsylvania in the midst of eleven meetings in ten days. I had finished ministering at an inner city house church and was one and a half hours from my next assignment, another home bible study on the Maryland border. I had time to kill and the memory of a diner I had visited a year or so ago came to mind. It would be the ideal place to relax and over indulge in diner goodness and coffee. Little did I know that I was walking into another divine appointment.

As I walked through the door of this diner, I was greeted and welcomed by the hostess as she showed me to my booth. A friendly young lady took my drink order and paused for a second to talk to a co-worker. Their conversation was highlighted to me as I waited for my drink. They were discussing work schedules and my waitress explained that she had worked fourteen hours that day so far, and she had worked out child care for her eight year old so she could finish the day at twenty hours. They wrapped up their conversation about single motherhood and dead beats dads and the lack of sleep they had.

I tried to keep my attention on the menu and the very

cheesy lasagna they offered, but now heaven was over riding my earthly preoccupation.

The Father began to tell me how proud he was of "His Girl". He spoke to me of how she worked the miraculous to juggle work, parenting and sleep. Then he began telling me about provision, opportunities and practical hope that he had planned to give her.

When she returned, I told her what Papa's heart was toward her and the change he was going to bring on her behalf. The fatigued young waitress brightened right in front of me, good news will do that to a person.
I never ate all my lasagna, the presence of God changed my appetite.

I've learned some things:

• God will meet you through your human senses to lead you to who or what he wants to speak to.
• He will let you hear things that are none of your business but is *HIS* business.
• Sometimes it is on the way, other times it is out of our way and may be an inconvenience - Luke 24:13-35.
• He sees and cares about human struggle. Religion has given God a bad reputation - that he is cold and indifferent to us. But Jesus is way different than religion - he is warm and caring.

Maybe the important things we are doing aren't as significant as the struggling person he leads us to.

When we listen, he will often tell us his heart for those around us.

Has Holy Spirit made you aware of others challenges when you were occupied with other things?

Do you recognize God's heart for people around you?

Do you ask Him to show you other's hearts?

3

PARDON THE INTERRUPTION

The first two stories illustrate a truth that I was slow to come to. Religion had taught me that Holy Spirit is always a gentle person. He is, but he interrupts me all the time. When I feel interrupted from what I was doing and taken on a different course, so to speak, it is more than likely the Spirit has an assignment for me.

I think, perhaps, I am way too ME oriented. Another component is that God looks for availability. First Thessalonians 5:19 says not to quench the spirit. Quench is like pouring water on a fire and the fire is put out. All too often indifference, distraction, worry, fear or self centeredness will do just that, quench Holy Spirit. When that happens, when we let things distract us from God, we become unavailable to God's purposes. He can, and often does, choose another to walk out the assignment we may have ignored or been clueless to.

Honestly, in my forty-seven year journey with Jesus, I have spent years where I believed I couldn't hear him. The problem was on my end. God was gracious to break through my diminished perception to reveal the simplicity of hearing him.
I mentor people who are hungry to consistently hear and obey God. A common challenge is that people often think they cannot hear or that God, because of their flaws, won't speak to them. This thought process is a lie from the enemy, the accuser of the brethren.

-Revelation 12:10. In John 10:27 it unequivocally states that if we are his, we hear his voice. As simple and straight forward as that!

Religion reduces hearing God to a quiet time or prayer closet experience. I get alone with God, but what I am outlining is that he is not content with that.
First Thessalonians 5:16-18 states that we are to pray without ceasing. We cannot stay in a prayer closet all day and night, we must learn that he is always with us and longs for that relationship of constant conversation. As a husband and wife, Cate and I have had a constant recurring conversation for forty-four years. Similarly, God longs for a constant relationship with us.

If you have a hunger to hear more from God, have your quiet time, however you prefer to do it. But expect God to interrupt your activities. He is pursuing our whole heart. I choose to be available when he calls.

Consider Psalms 46:10-11, "Cease striving and know that I am God; I will be exalted among the nations, I will be exalted in the earth. The Lord of hosts is with us; the God of Jacob is our stronghold."
In these verses, stillness appears to lead to awareness of his presence and our security.

Name some God interruptions you have experienced.

Have you experienced being still before God?

In what ways and in what settings are you most aware of His presence?

4

LESS OF ME

How we perceive God will influence how much of his kingdom we receive. That statement may offend the beliefs of some. However, as the rest of my stories catalogue, I have interacted with God over the last forty-seven years. Those years and encounters have given me lessons that I pass on to you.

I had many limiting and hindering beliefs. Hurt and disappointment, that I had kept, became big road blocks to experiencing everything God possessed for me.

At this time, I was an intern at a large ministry centered around prayer. We spent hours each day in prayer for others, studying the subject of prayer, and serving others. After thirty-one years of pastoral ministry, Cate and I felt directed to a season in this environment. Sustaining us in this place were part-time jobs and the faithful contributions of partners to our ministry. With all that, the living obligations for each month were more than the resources on hand.

One particular day, when my limited view of God convinced me that we were a sinking ship, love broke in. During a meeting in an out of the way conference room, sixty-three of us interns gathered with twelve staff members who were training us in the prayer lifestyle when we were visited by an anonymous gentleman. He made some discreet inquiries of how many of us were in the training and how many were staff. He observed the session and then departed.

What we were pursuing, and how we went about it, was something that raises peoples interest. That was probably the reason that no one who observed our visitor thought anything of it.

The next morning, the same gentleman reappeared with a bag and with instructions of how the contents were to be distributed to the seventy-five people in the room. My view of God was about to be broken open.

My typical week consisted of twenty-four hours of part-time work on a midnight shift at a mental health crisis center. Another forty-eight hours a week, over six days, was invested in my training to be an intercessor for the kingdom of God. My candle burned at both ends. Add financial pressure and I frequently felt overwhelmed. I was aware of God, but I couldn't always see him.

The bag in question contained $50,000 in cash. Per our anonymous friend, an envelope for each, with a portion, was distributed the next day.

Our monthly short fall for that month was gone. Something was shattered, it was my unbelieving view of what and how God would break in.

The money went for needs, but the deep need in my heart was satisfied. Matthew 5:3 - The Message:
"You're blessed when you're at the end of your rope. With less of you there is more of God and his rule."

Are you often more aware of challenges than you are of God?

What are some activities that awake your awareness of Him?

Name an occasion that God met a need in a totally unexpected way.

5

WHEN BEAUTY CAME IN

He is the God who is beautiful. Isaiah 28:5 - "In that day the Lord Almighty will be a glorious crown, a beautiful wreath for the remnant of his people."

Psalm 27:4 - "One thing I ask of the Lord. This is what I seek - that I may dwell in the house of the Lord all the days of my life, to gaze upon the beauty of the Lord......"

Before I knew the Lord, the beauty of his creation amazed me in the scenery of Lake Coeur d'Alene Idaho, where I grew up. And the hundreds of lakes I saw while riding a train across northern Ontario were breathtaking.

The most memorable experience was the north shore of Kauai, Hawaii, months before I gave my heart to Christ. The stunning beaches, the powerful waves rolling onto the shore, the crystal waterfalls and pools, and the surf sounding as loud as a freight train as it crashed onto the beach. Seeing all this beauty with my eyes only produced wonderful memories of great beauty - but it didn't fill my heart.

Even after I had known God for decades I didn't yet understand that the God of creation loves to release his beauty into every situation of our life. It's another perception of his desire to commune with us.

Cate and I, accompanied by our son, Matthias and his wife Tineke, were in Waverley Station, Edinburgh Scotland a few days before Christmas 2017. The cold outside had brought us into the very full and beautiful waiting room. The architecture of this room reminded me of a cathedral rather than a transportation hub. Highly polished floors, wooden walls and a high glass ceiling, even pigeons walking around hoping for a handout. In the center was a baby grand piano, keyboard open and ready.

We awaited the announcement for which of the eighteen platforms we would need to rush to when it was time to depart. The electronic sign up high on the wall opposite us, the crowds of people heading to work and holiday destinations all spoke of tension and busyness.

But all of that soon washed away as melodic notes began to fill the room with beautiful music.

Three different talented people took their place at the piano as they also were waiting for a train. The train station was transformed into a concert hall. Classical music, Christmas Carols and one young lady sang as she took her turn at the piano. The background noises seemed to disappear as I watched the atmosphere change.

What you need to understand is that -
• There was no schedule of performers. The players were walking along, suitcases in tow, and simply stopped and played
• The piano had no "DO NOT TOUCH" sign on it
• Each player made a decision to take a risk
• So many things could go wrong with such spontaneity

But Beauty entered the room. Our yuletide concert was the entry point to touch deep places in many lives, if they allowed. Someone made room for Him to enter, and he did.

Understand that life often doesn't serve up the beauty, quite the opposite, some ordinary people made room for the beauty to come and he came on that ordinary, busy day just before Christmas, 2017.

I think the human need to control situations and time works against us. When we control our lives, simply because we don't trust anyone else to work it out or to work with us, we shut out the beauty that is always around us. The scripture sited previously, Psalms 27:4, indicates that David had become preoccupied and centered on beauty - the beauty of God, that is.

Our life story illustrates what can happen when we make room for beauty. It is risky, but the bigger risk is not to make that room.

Are you regularly aware of beauty around you?

Have you had an experience of beauty coming to your everyday norm?

Have you tried gazing on beauty as David did?

Patrick G. Bryson

6

PERCEPTION

The Relevant point is where we are in relation to the light. We were born with a disposition for darkness. That was our original order.

We were created for light. Illumination, transparency and exposure are characteristics of the Children of Light. Ephesians 5:8 states, "For you were formally darkness, but now you are light in the Lord; walk as children of light".

What brings us from our original fallen state to what he intended is the change that happens when we trust him. That moment, the transformative millisecond, if you will, changes everything in our journey.

What was unseen to my eyes and undisclosed to any of my senses, before that moment, was the reality of God's person and his love. My sight and all means of perception were transformed in that moment.

Someone might think I am making much of what can happen in a moment. That is one of a myriad of amazing characteristics of Christ's Kingdom, that very moment.

The transformation I am speaking of brings us into alignment with he throne of the universe and beyond. What I could never earn or buy is now available to me as an amazing gift.

So life is now oriented around drawing near to him and his heart for others. Read Psalms 73:28 and John 15:12-15. These verses speak of a place of liberty; loving others with the love that the Father gives me.

I have found that much of the experience of most church going people is not like this. Religion has added layers of expectations, rules, methods, and programs that draw us away from simplicity.

In the time frame of my writing this I have a renewed understanding of the need to let go of any and all things that draw me away from this simple truth.

Have you felt constrained by religious expectations?

Do you ever feel conflicted by what Holy Spirit is leading and religious demands?

7

CHICKEN DELIGHT

My focus was a chicken sandwich from a fast food restaurant next to our motel in Birmingham, Alabama. Twelve hours of driving, beginning at three in the morning, had brought us here for the night. Now chicken delight and then sleep was my focus.

On entering the establishment a nice young man greeted me from behind the counter. After pleasantries and his taking my order he looked at me and asked, "Say, are you a professor at the University?" I pleaded innocent to that charge, however, I did confess to being guilty of being a minister. The young man was excited by my confession. "I go to Marvel Christian, it's a great church. Have you heard of it?" I told my new found brother that I was just passing through and had not heard of his church.

A female customer was gathering napkins and straws for her order when she told me that she too, was visiting the area. She went on and told me she had just had a large tumor removed from her throat and was in the best health she had been in for years and she said she had Jesus to thank for that.

I now felt gripped by the spirit of God. I began to declare to her that the purpose of God was not merely to survive but to live in freedom and boldness. He wanted her to know she was given a gift and how she had thought she might not have this time. Now God wanted her to redeem the time by making the most of every opportunity.

The devil had failed. His intent was death, BUT GOD! My my new friend, Margie, was stepping on the enemy's plans not just for herself but for whoever God brought her way. And last of all, that she was not to look back at past mistakes, but instead to live in intimate friendship with her King.

God is so good at what he does. I desired chicken and he was serving something else that day in the fast food restaurant. He was serving hope and encouragement to hearts. Margie, the young man behind the counter and myself were a part of a larger drama.

II Thessalonians 3:5 comes to mind, "May the Lord direct your hearts into the love of God and into the steadfastness of Christ." Sometimes I think the fulfillment of this verse to be mystical, a light appearing and us having warm fuzzies with persistence added. In my case, the directing of my heart was the vehicle of a desire for spicy chicken on a bun. I believe Margie had a similar desire. The young man at the counter asked what he thought was an innocent question and heaven invaded the room. God's spirit, the spirit of prophecy and Holy Spirit orchestrated all three of us into a holy moment.

I live and strive for awareness of what God is doing around me. Even when I am unaware, he leads me.

How aware are you of God "setting up situations" to speak to you or through you?

Invite God to give you divine appointments and awareness to see them.

8

BEYOND EXPECTATIONS

It was 1987, I was a thirty-eight year old discouraged pastor.   The past year in our ministry at a non-denominational church in the mountains of central California we had dealt with spiritual warfare, division and stress.   The five previous years my wife and I had attended a yearly pastors conference at a large pentecostal church in the Los Angeles area.   This year the decrease in church funds caused me to attend only one day out of the five, and without my wife.

It was a Wednesday night meeting, meaning that in addition to the fifteen hundred pastors present for the conference there were also the regular parishioners in attendance.   I arrived early, knowing the attendance would be very large and parking difficult.

After a brief discussion with the brother who was attending with me, we decided to visit the on campus book store.   In my mind I was looking forward to hearing the internationally known Korean pastor who was speaking that night.

At this time in my life I had certain ways I expected God to minister to me.   I had him in a box and controlled that box rather nicely, at least I thought so.   My discouragement and weariness added to my perception that God would only come to me in a few prescribed avenues.

As I entered the store I walked by the elevated area

where the cash registers and workers were busily helping the overflowing crowd of customers. I noticed a man standing near the registers wearing a store managers badge as he made eye contact with me. I busied myself with looking at books I wanted but could not afford at this time.

After a time of looking at theology books, biographies and fiction works I became restless. The store manager, all of a sudden, was beside me. I had no conference tag on and he started a conversation by saying, "You're a pastor." I admitted I was. He then said, "There are some things you need." He had five books in his hands and I started to tell him I just couldn't afford them at this time when he interrupted me. He told me it was all taken care of as he turned toward the register and had them bagged up. I briefly looked at the books but kept them in the bag and went to the main hall for the main speaker.

I no longer remember what the speaker spoke of that night. My problems didn't go away. In fact, a year later we had resigned pastoring and moved to Los Angeles. But the books that man handed me! God came to me in those books. Testimonies, biblical wisdom, practical insight, comfort and understanding came to me in those books. One man, sensitive to Holy Spirit in a busy environment heard God and was his messenger when I needed it more than I knew.

I want to be just like that store manager, sensitive when pressures and demands all around me resist. I want to hear what is needed for those around me. I want to prophesy with actions as he paid for the books, gave his time and honored me.

Our big God, our amazing God wants to come to us in ways and means that we haven't seen yet.

Does busyness and pressure prevent you from seeing what God is doing in others?

Thought: His presence is available abundantly when you are feeling pressure. Psalm 46:1

Patrick G. Bryson

9

GO BANANAS

I was suppose to buy the cheaper bananas, or was I? Urgent things to be done as a dual vocational person - pastor and sales manager - sometimes took much of my time causing me to leave work too late to get the better deal.

It was nearly sunset on a summer weekend in Cape May County, New Jersey. Our county of ninety thousand residents took on about four hundred thousand extra people in the summer. I had received a call from Cate, plenty early, to pick up bananas from a members discount store near the office on the way home. I left after it closed and knew I had to face the throngs at the local market and end up paying more for those bananas.

I love that our God sees the whole picture even if I never do. I was juggling bananas as I got into the very long check-out line. It was then that I saw her, the lady in front of me that I almost didn't recognize. She had visited our small church only a few times. As I stood there a few words bubbled up inside me, "Love's labour's lost", which I recognized as an early Shakespearean piece.

I knew it was a word for her. I didn't understand it and I wrestled with Holy Spirit for a moment, as well as the bananas.

I got her attention and we exchanged pleasantries

before I gave her the worlds I heard. Immediately upon speaking them out she was touched within. Tears came to her eyes as she grabbed my arm saying, "Thank you, that means so much."

I payed too much for the bananas, but I had a Divine appointment in the check out lane of a very crowded local market. I did not understand the the word or what it meant to her, but she did. The receiver is the only one who needs to get the meaning.

The delays and distractions served only to have me in the right place at the right time to see the right person. God is genius. He knows what he is doing and hearing his voice and obeying it will take us on adventures in the mundaneness of ordinary days.

Do you believe you must understand what God gives you before sharing with others?

Thought: We sometime receive sealed messages for others. Even if we see it, it isn't for us to understand but deliver.

10

A MEETING WITH GOD

I was minding my own business a half hour before the start of a church service. The twenty-four hundred seat auditorium was virtually empty. Cate and I had arrived early and were seated on the side section, about twelve rows from the front. My strategy in sitting here was to see the platform well but still be able to leave in a timely manner at the end of the service.

My point of focus was what would happen on the platform - worship team, preaching, altar calls. I was a pastor so I was sure I knew how things would work.

The seats were still mostly empty when she arrived. She entered the back of the sanctuary, looked around and walked down the aisle and sat down next to me. I noticed that she was professional in appearance and walked confidently to the seat next to me as if it were assigned to her.

We rarely notice when destiny enters the room and sits right next to us. At least that is true of me on that night in 1984. When the service began every seat and overflow room was full. Worship was powerful and then the announcements were made. The pastor came to the pulpit and invited us all into prayer for one another. We were instructed to break up in groups of four or five. Cate paired with another lady seated in front of her. The lady next to me said, "You are a pastor, this is the word of the Lord. You are a Joshua person, God will be with you every day of your life. He will not forsake you. You will bring God's people into their inheritance, even one by one. Be strong and of good courage. He will not fail you....". Immediately after she told me this she left.

The prayer time was over and the pastor preached but I didn't hear. My eyes stayed filled with tears and my heart was in awe. I wrote down this word in the margins of my bible so I could ponder it. You see, I couldn't grasp it completely because it was outside the boundaries I had formed of how I see God. The church I pastored was small and I felt inadequate in my love for Cate and our children. I just couldn't grasp her words completely since I felt so small and thought so small of my God.

Over the years I questioned this word and this word has chastened me, challenged me, and it also called me closer to God. I have tried to let it go, put it aside, but it has never let go me me.

I had never gotten to speak with his messenger from that day and never knew who she was, but through that encounter I have gotten closer to God. He is always looking to strengthen shaky and uncertain hearts. He never comes to us on the basis of performance but through providence. This was a moment, an important moment, in his persuading me of his goodness and kindness towards me. A word I needed for change.

Has destiny ever entered the room and sat next to you? Write down your experience with destiny - God still has something to say from your experience.

Are you aware that God is pursuing you, even in lack of understanding and weakness?

Patrick G. Bryson

11

GOD SENT HIS WORD

Years had gone by and I hadn't talked to him, things were okay when we parted. I was his sales manager, we had won awards together and I had been salesman of the year in our region, and then a top sales manager for his water treatment company for several years. He was a sincere christian, a good employer and he had a kindness in his dealings with me. God moved me on.

I was now working as a teacher at a private high school during the day and at an adult mental health group home in the evenings.

My days were busy. I was driving to a gas station when the word for my former boss came to my spirit, "He's choosing investments, tell him if he invests in the Kingdom he will receive his best return."

I was the reluctant prophet. We hadn't spoken recently and I knew he was hard to get a hold of since he operated offices in three states. My human nature wasn't comfortable with obeying God.

I called his cell, which was usually answered by a secretary, he answered. We exchanged pleasantries, caught up on children, business, our latest pursuits. I then told him the word which was followed by a long silence on his end. He then said, "Do you know what I'm doing right now?" I said I did not.

He replied that he was considering two potential

investments. One was a mutual fund and the other was a christian organization that dug wells in Africa to provide safe water supply. That word blew his mind.

That word came to me almost like my own thoughts, but they came to my spirit before being processed in my mind - I Thessalonians 5:23. Experience has taught me, and I am still learning, to recognize and respond to this heavenly input.

The plan is that it is true that God knows every detail of your life, what is on your plate or on your desk, as well as what you desire. He says that he will instruct you and teach you, he will guide you with his eye -Psalms 32:8.

Such experiences are to be normal for a believer. The word I received demonstrates the father's love for his child. In the moment wisdom was needed, God sent his word.

Are you reluctant to respond to Holy Spirit promptings?

If so, Why? Is it awkward?

Thought: I have found that God likes awkward! Just because it is awkward doesn't mean it isn't God!

12

NO MORE A SKEPTIC

I was a skeptic. It was 1983 and John Wimber was a modern day reformer. He invited the church to experience the demonstration and power of Holy Spirit, especially in healing. He was both reformer and teacher and I had heard him speak on several occasions.

He was scheduled to speak at a large Baptist Church in Bakersfield, California. I invited my church leaders to come as well, all that to say I still had my doubts and I held onto them tight.

The church was packed on a hot August day when the speaker, after a short message with biblical references, announced, "Holy Spirit is coming in the room like a wind".

That statement hit my skeptic's button hard. How did he know what Holy Spirit was doing? I was turning this over in my mind when a warm blanket feeling wrapped around me. I felt like I was floating. I was standing at the front of the church along with hundreds of others when a young intern, who accompanied John Wimber, made her way to my side. She placed her hands on my shoulder and began to speak an end to my fears and doubts.

By word of knowledge she identified my specific fears and doubts. I was so overcome with the realization that my very thoughts were exposed to this woman, by Holy

Spirit, that I could hardly stand. Heaviness, insecurity and doubt lifted off of me. I felt Holy Spirit rest on me for quite a while and I no longer was a skeptic. The Good Shepherd rescued me from the cliff of my doubts.

Take a few moments and write down an overwhelming encounter you have had with God.

Did you see a difference in the presence of fear or doubt after your encounter?

13

SUMMATION

I have wandered and I have doubted. I have spent years in discouragement. In every instance God came to me, sovereignly, through other people, or a song or even a billboard. He has always come to me.

In all this, I have become persuaded of the paramount, infinite goodness - Exodus 34 - , mercy, kindness, love, compassion - I Corinthians 13 - and wisdom - Proverbs 2 & 3 - of God!

My perspective has changed. I now expect him. Specifically, I expect him to be present in all of life. I have gone from a belief in a God who would occasionally show himself to knowing the God who is abundantly available in tight places - Psalms 46:1.

My life has been moving forward. I used to spend a lot of time being preoccupied with my circumstances. More and more I am preoccupied with him.

I love the body of Christ - everyone who names his name as savior and trusts him. I am not fond of religion which seeks to control and direct how God deals with His bride. The living relationship he has made available to us through faith can never be contained in a program, system, church politics and ego driven activities.

Church is his family, it is our opportunity to serve in, and with, his living representatives on earth. When the

bride (church) learns her place as his beloved, we are no longer just holding meetings.
God is taking away the things that hinder us from seeing him for who he really is. Isaiah 9:6 - And his name shall be called Wonderful, Counselor, Mighty God, Eternal Father, Prince of Peace.

David, in Psalm 27:4, said he wanted to dwell in the house (family) of the Lord , gaze on God's beauty and inquire (ask questions of His heart) in His presence.

Inquire about:

His vast love for you

His good plans

His purpose in your present situation

His destiny (ultimate results) of your life

Consider taking a few days with each question.

Patrick G. Bryson

ABOUT THE AUTHOR

Patrick Bryson is available for mentoring in hearing the voice of God in your personal life, business, church leadership and group meetings.
He resides with his wife, Cathy, and their two dogs in Warrensburg, Missouri
www.patandcatebryson.com
patandcatebryson@gmail.com

Made in the
USA
Lexington, KY